Hawk Mother

The Story of a Red-tailed Hawk
Who Hatched Chickens

KARA HAGEDORN

Web of Life

CHILDREN'S BOOKS

One moment, the red-tailed hawk is soaring through the sky. The next moment, she is tumbling to the ground. In that moment, she has lost her freedom.

More About Hawks

Over 200 species of hawks are found worldwide. They live in every habitat except for the North and South Poles. In Europe, Africa and Asia, they are often called buzzards.

Seventeen species of hawks can be found in North America. The red-tailed hawk is the most common hawk in the United States and Canada and is easy to identify. On warm days you may notice red-tailed hawks circling in the sky, spreading their bright red tails. Or when traveling in your car you may see them perching on the tops of telephone poles, where they sit patiently looking for rodents, insects, snakes, rabbits and other animals to eat.

Some farmers call red-tailed hawks "chicken hawks" because they blame the hawks for killing their chickens. Although hawks will sometimes kill young chickens if the chickens stray too far from the coop, chickens are more likely to be victims of a sly fox, raccoon or weasel raiding their coop. Farmers have sometimes shot or poisoned red-tailed hawks without realizing that the hawks actually help to protect crops from hungry mice and rabbits.

Today, many countries have laws to protect hawks. In the United States all birds of prey are protected under the Migratory Bird Treaty Act. Unfortunately, despite these protections, many hawks like Sunshine are still illegally shot. To find out more about hawks and how you can help protect them, contact the organizations listed below.

Birdlife International www.birdlife.org

The National Audubon Society www.audubon.org

Royal Society for the Protection of Birds www.rspb.org.uk

Sunshine and Kara's Story

Sunshine and I have been friends for over twenty years. Because of my degree in zoology and my experience working at the Cornell University Hawk Barn, I was able to qualify for the necessary permits to become Sunshine's caretaker. I spent many hours training Sunshine, and together we have given hundreds of presentations in schools, parks and libraries, educating thousands of people about the importance of protecting birds in the wild.

When I adopted Sunshine, I made a serious commitment to care for her knowing that hawks can live for over 30 years in captivity. I'm guessing she was around three years old when I adopted her because she had the red tail of an adult but the pale yellow eyes of a juvenile.

Sunshine finds favorite perching places all over the yard and we spend time together every day. Over time Sunshine and I have learned to communicate through body language so that I can tell if she is hot or cold, hungry, irritated, bored, excited, relaxed or ready to go to sleep in her aviary.

Sunshine teaches me to be more patient and observant. She gives a rasping call to let me know if a cat is in the yard. She turns an eye to the sky and I suddenly notice a golden eagle soaring overhead. She alerts me to a lizard on the trunk of a tree by staring at it.

Adopting Sunshine has transformed my life, and I am happy that I was able to enrich her life by helping her become a mother. Each spring, I still help Sunshine build a nest and incubate eggs.

Sunshine surprised us all by mothering chickens just like they were her very own. If she had found them in the wild she would have eaten them. That's what hawks do. But since she hatched them herself she gave them all the care and protection they needed until they were fully grown. With my help, Sunshine persevered through her injury and loss of freedom and was finally able to become a parent. Sunshine's inspiring story shows how we can all overcome challenges and adjust to new situations with the help of others!

For a few days Sunshine wanders around the yard looking for the chickens. She goes to all their favorite places holding food in her sharp bill, ready to feed them. But eventually she realizes they are gone. If Sunshine were in the wild, her young hawks would also leave the nest to find a new home.

Roosters are too noisy for my neighbors so I have to find them a new home. I take Gaia and Sage to my friend's farm where they will be surrounded by horses, sheep and other chickens. They can spend the day out in the yard and then have a safe **coop** to **roost** in at night.

Gaia and Sage are healthy and well cared for and grow rapidly.
After two months, they are as big as Sunshine! One morning, at dawn,
they begin to crow. They are both grown-up roosters now!

Sunshine is very gentle with the chicks and never steps on them with her big feet or sharp talons. The chicks follow Sunshine out to the yard to perch in the sun.

The chicks continue to grow but always stay close to their mother.
At night, they crawl under her to keep warm.

I name the chicks Gaia and Sage. I feed them chicken grain and Sunshine shares her meat with them.

But, instead, Sunshine jumps down and grabs a snake with her sharp **talons**! She is hunting for the chicks' first meal! Even though chicks don't normally eat snakes, they run right over and peck the meat from Sunshine's bill. To my great relief I realize the chicks will be safe. Sunshine knows the chicks are her young even though they don't look or act like hawk chicks. And the chicks know Sunshine is their mother even though she doesn't scratch and peck at the ground like a hen would do.

That night I try to sleep, but instead I toss and turn wondering what will happen. I know that by **instinct** Sunshine would expect her young to be in the nest with their mouths open, waiting for her to feed them. But when I wake up the next morning the baby chicks are already on the ground foraging in the grass!

Then I see a sharp look in Sunshine's eye. It's a look I've seen many times before. She has spotted **prey**—something to eat—and she is about to jump down to grab it.

I freeze with fear and think, *She's going to eat the chicks!*

I am so happy that after all these years Sunshine finally has young! But now I am worried that Sunshine won't accept these chicks as her own because baby chickens and baby hawks behave very differently from each other. Baby chickens are able to stand and walk around soon after they are born. They can even **forage** for food on their own. But baby hawks are born helpless. They need their parents to take care of them: protecting them, keeping them warm and feeding them until they can fly on their own.

I check on the eggs throughout the day as the cracks get bigger. By sunset both chicks have hatched and are **brooding** under Sunshine's warm breast!

And then one day, near the end of April, Sunshine will not get off her nest. Then I hear a peep! Sunshine hears it, too. Her eyes light up with excitement! One of the chicks has begun to break through the egg's shell with its **egg tooth**.

I lift Sunshine from the nest and replace her infertile eggs with two fertile chicken eggs. I'm not sure how she will react, but she doesn't seem to notice the difference. She sits right down and incubates them. We work together every day to keep the eggs warm and the nest neat and tidy.

The neighbors bring me a basket of eggs to choose from. There are many beautiful colors. I pick two pale blue eggs because they look the most like hawk eggs.

It makes me sad that a gun took away Sunshine's freedom to fly, find a mate and raise her young. I wish I could help her. And then one spring, I have an idea! I ask our neighbors to bring me two chicken eggs. On their farm, they have a rooster named Bart, so I know the eggs will be **fertile**.

Every spring for seven years we share this routine of building a nest and taking turns watching over the eggs. But Sunshine's eggs are always infertile and they will never hatch. Each year I eventually have to take away her eggs and tear up the nest. Sunshine seems confused when I do this, but if I don't tear up the nest she will sit on the eggs all summer waiting for them to hatch.

Now that Sunshine has laid two eggs, she expects me to help her. In the wild, both the male and female hawks take care of the eggs. One parent keeps the eggs warm while the other parent gets up and leaves the nest to stretch, hunt and eat. Several times a day I walk into the aviary and quietly approach the nest. Sunshine hops off her nest and I cover the eggs with my hands to keep them warm.

Several weeks later Sunshine lays two eggs! I know the eggs are **infertile** because Sunshine does not have a **mate**. The eggs will never hatch into chicks. But Sunshine sits on them anyway to **incubate** them, keeping them warm as if there are chicks growing inside.

One spring, to my surprise, Sunshine carries a clump of grass to her aviary and starts to build a nest. In the wild, male and female hawks build the nest together, but Sunshine is alone. She looks at me and I know she wants me to help. I bring her sticks, moss and leaves. She works for hours moving things around until the nest is just right.

I let Sunshine be as wild as possible. I build her a big **aviary** where she can get fresh air and watch other birds. Every day I help her out into the yard so she can bathe in the rain or stretch her broken wing in the warm sunlight. She hunts lizards and gophers and watches the neighborhood hawks circle in the sky above her. She calls out to them in a rasping territorial scream, "Kleeeer! Kleeeer!"

The hawk is taken to the wildlife center where I work. Because I am a **zoologist**, I am allowed to take care of her. She is patient and calm even though she is wounded and in pain. We name her "Sunshine" because of her bright personality. Sunshine and I become friends. Eventually I am able to adopt her and bring her home with me. I train her to sit on my gloved hand. Every day Sunshine and I become more comfortable with each other.

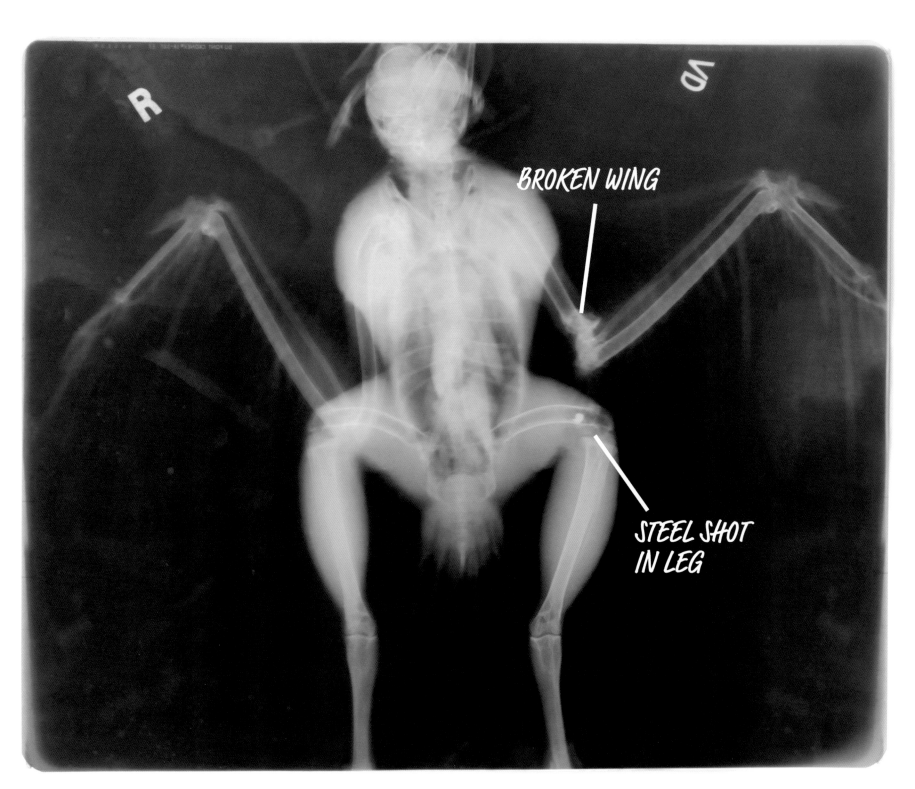

BROKEN WING

STEEL SHOT
IN LEG

A man finds the hawk lying in a field. She is starving and wounded. Her left wing is broken. The man carefully wraps her in a blanket and takes her to a **veterinarian**.

An X-ray shows the hawk has been shot. She will never be able to soar freely through the skies again. The hawk can no longer hunt for food or protect herself. In order for her to stay alive and healthy, people will need to take care of her.

Glossary

aviary - large structure designed for birds to live in

brooding - sitting on eggs or chicks to keep them warm

coop - cage or pen for small animals

egg tooth - sharp growth on the nose or beak of a baby bird that it uses to break through the shell of its egg when hatching

fertile - able to grow a baby chick inside it

forage - search for food

incubate - keep eggs warm until it is time for them to hatch

infertile - not able to grow a baby chick inside it

instinct - natural behavior an animal is born with that it doesn't have to learn

mate - one of a pair of animals that has babies together

prey - animal being hunted, caught and eaten by another animal

roost - rest or sleep on something high above the ground such as a tree branch or a wooden perch

talons - sharp, pointed claws on the feet of a bird of prey

veterinarian - doctor who treats animals

zoologist - person who specializes in the study or science of animals

In memory of Rob Kimmell, who provided the chicken
eggs from Tread Lightly Farm. —K.H.

A very special thanks to wildlife rehabilitator Jean Soprano and veterinarian
Alison Hazel, who encouraged me to adopt Sunshine, and to my publisher Madeleine Dunphy
who motivated me to hatch this story and send it out into the world. And deep love to my
husband, Yarrow Nelson, who tolerates rats in the freezer.

Photo Acknowledgments: The images in this book are used with the permission of
the copyright holders: Feathers courtesy of Sunshine, title page; © Vic Berardi, pp. 2-3;
© Kara Hagedorn, front cover, pp. 4, 8, 9, 10, 11, 12 (inset), 13, 16, 17, 18, 19, 20, 21, 22, 23, 24,
25, 26, 28; © Yarrow Nelson, p. 7; © Glenn Forbes, pp. 12 (top), 15, 27; photo by Rob Kimmell,
© Karyn Kimmell, p. 14; © Jay Waddel, p. 29; © Eva Vigil, back cover.

Book design by Philip Krayna, Modiv Design, www.modiv.design

Published in the United States in 2017 by Web of Life Children's Books, Berkeley, California.
Second printing 2017. Third printing 2018. First paperback edition: 2024.

Library of Congress Control Number: 2016960153
ISBN: 978-0-9883303-7-5 (hardcover edition)
ISBN: 978-1-970039-07-8 (paperback edition)

Printed in China by Toppan Leefung Printing

For free, downloadable activities, and for more information about our books and the authors
and artists who created them, visit our website: www.weboflifebooks.com

Distributed by Publishers Group West
(800) 788-3123 • www.pgw.com